THE SEMINOLE WARS

ELLIS ROXBURGH

Gareth Stevens
PUBLISHING

Please visit our website, www.garethstevens.com. For a free color catalog of all our high-quality books, call toll-free 1-800-542-2595 or fax 1-877-542-2596.

CATALOGING-IN-PUBLICATION DATA

Names: Roxburgh, Ellis.
Title: The Seminole Wars / Ellis Roxburgh.
Description: New York : Gareth Stevens Publishing, 2018. | Series: Rebellions, revolts, and uprisings | Includes index.
Identifiers: ISBN 9781538207734 (pbk.) | ISBN 9781538207673 (library bound) | ISBN 9781538207550 (6 pack)
Subjects: LCSH: Seminole Indians--Wars. | Seminole War, 1st, 1817-1818. | Seminole War, 2nd, 1835-1842. | Seminole War, 3rd, 1855-1858.
Classification: LCC E83.817 R69 2018 | DDC 973.5'7--dc23

Published in 2018 by
Gareth Stevens Publishing
111 East 14th Street, Suite 349
New York, NY 10003

For Brown Bear Books Ltd:
Managing Editor: Tim Cooke
Designer: Lynne Lennon
Editorial Director: Lindsey Lowe
Children's Publisher: Anne O'Daly
Design Manager: Keith Davis
Picture Manager: Sophie Mortimer

Picture Credits
Cover: Getty: MPI, Archive Photos
Interior: Alamy: Vanessa Grossemy 31; Dreamstime: John Anderson 14; istockphoto: 29; Library of Congress: 5, 8, 9, 10, 11, 13, 18, 22, 23, 24, 26, 27, 28, 30, 34, 36, 42, 43; National Archives: 16, 19, Indian Gallery/War Department 39; Public Domain: Intergalactic 6, New York Public Library 17, Saint Louis Art Museum 41, si.edu 12, Smithsonian American Art Museum 32, West Point Museum of Art 35, Zazzle 33; Shutterstock: 40, Alocdesign 37, Everett Historical 4, Zack Frank 21; Thinkstock: istockphoto 7, 20, 38, Liquid Library 15.

All other images Brown Bear Books

Brown Bear Books has made every attempt to contact the copyright holder.
If anyone has any information please contact licensing@brownbearbooks.co.uk

Manufactured in the United States of America

CPSIA compliance information: Batch #CS17GS. For further information contact Gareth Stevens, New York, New York at 1-800-542-2595.

CONTENTS

WORDS IN THE GLOSSARY APPEAR IN **BOLD** TYPE
THE FIRST TIME THEY ARE USED IN THE TEXT.

ROOTS OF REBELLION

Between 1817 and 1858, Native Americans fought three separate wars against the United States in Florida. These Seminole Wars were the longest of all Native American wars against the US government.

The Seminole Wars had two main causes. One was slavery, and the other was US expansion over the North American continent. The first European settlers in Florida were Spanish. Slavery was an established practice in southern Spain. Since the first **conquistadors** had sailed across the Atlantic Ocean, the Spaniards had brought slaves to the Americas. Slavery under the Spaniards was different

→

Slave traders split up an African family after the father is sold into slavery in the United States.

4

from slavery elsewhere in North America. Under Spanish law, slaves were allowed to own property and transfer it as they wanted. They also had legal rights, including the right to self-purchase. This gave a slave who had saved enough money the right to pay off his or her master. Many slaves used this right of self-purchase to buy their freedom. A class of free blacks existed first in Spain and then in Spanish America.

Settling Florida

The first Spaniard in Florida was Juan Ponce de Léon, who claimed the region for Spain in 1513. In 1565, Spain founded a fort in St. Augustine. It is now the oldest continually occupied European settlement in the United States.

Hernando de Soto brought African slaves to Florida in 1539.

SPAIN'S SANCTUARY POLICY

IN 1693, SPAIN WAS INCREASING ITS SETTLEMENT OF FLORIDA. TO ATTRACT MORE SETTLERS, IT INTRODUCED A POLICY THAT STATED THAT ANY SLAVE WHO MOVED TO FLORIDA AND CONVERTED TO CATHOLICISM WOULD BE GRANTED HIS OR HER FREEDOM. THE PROMISE ATTRACTED A FLOW OF BLACK IMMIGRANTS FROM THE NORTH. ENGLAND'S COLONY IN CAROLINA OBJECTED TO THE POLICY, BECAUSE SO MANY OF ITS SLAVES FLED SOUTH. IN THE EARLY 1800S, THE NEWLY FORMED UNITED STATES ALSO BECAME INCREASINGLY WORRIED ABOUT THE POLICY.

Florida was part of Spain's Caribbean territories for nearly 300 years before the United States took control in 1821 (Florida was briefly under British rule from 1763 to 1784). Under the Spanish, Florida developed differently from the English **colonies** to the north, which became US states in 1776. Slaves in Florida received better treatment than their neighbors in other states. By the early 1700s, many black slaves in Georgia and the Carolinas had escaped from their masters to Florida. There, the Spanish authorities allowed them to stay if they converted to the Catholic religion.

← The Spaniards built Fort Matanzas to guard St. Augustine.

The Spanish let escaped slaves and freed African Americans organize their own social and economic activities. The former slaves had far more freedom than they had farther north. They even served in Spanish **militias**.

A Challenge

From 1763 until the end of the Revolutionary War in 1784, the British seized temporary control of Florida. The British government wanted British people to move there.

Large parts of central Florida were covered in semitropical swamps. ↓

This was the treasury of Spanish Florida in St. Augustine.

←

The British gave settlers their own land. The new settlers needed slaves to work their land. The freedoms that had been enjoyed by Florida's slaves and freed blacks were over. Life became harsher. The British brought slaves from Sierra Leone in West Africa to work on **plantations**.

British rule was short-lived, however. At the end of the Revolutionary War, Florida was returned to Spanish control. The change led to chaos. Many slaves in Florida took the chance to escape from their British owners. They fled from the plantations and went to live with the Seminole people who lived on the central plains of northern Florida.

DID YOU KNOW?
THE BRITISH ORIGINALLY TOOK CONTROL OF FLORIDA FROM SPAIN IN 1763 AS PART OF A WIDER EUROPEAN CONFLICT KNOWN AS THE SEVEN YEARS' WAR.

Various Native American peoples had moved to Florida in the early 1700s to avoid wars farther north. These **refugees** came from several different tribes, including the Creek. In Florida they mingled with local Native peoples, such as the Choctaw. A new band emerged, known as the Seminole.

Pressure from the New Government

Under Spanish rule from 1784 to 1821, the numbers of freed blacks and slaves in Florida grew. The British who remained in Florida usually owned a large number of slaves. A typical plantation owner might have between 50 and 200 slaves. Generations of the same slave family worked on a plantation.

Spanish troops defeat the British at Pensacola in 1784, taking back control of Florida.

THE WAR OF 1812

IN 1812, THE UNITED STATES WENT TO WAR WITH GREAT BRITAIN AND ITS ALLIES. ONE CAUSE WAS BRITAIN'S ATTEMPTS TO RECRUIT AMERICANS INTO ITS NAVY IN EUROPE. BRITAIN ALSO LENT ITS SUPPORT TO NATIVE AMERICANS FIGHTING AGAINST THE UNITED STATES, AND IMPOSED RESTRICTIONS ON US TRADE. THE 3-YEAR WAR ENDED IN A STALEMATE AFTER THE BATTLE OF NEW ORLEANS IN 1815.

Andrew Jackson (center) commands US forces in the Battle of New Orleans in the War of 1812.

The newly formed United States government became worried about the large numbers of African Americans in Florida. It feared that the former slaves might try and rise up against their masters. The US government asked Spain to end its policy of giving **sanctuary** to runaway slaves.

In 1790, Spain ended its policy of religious sanctuary. Slaves who had already escaped to Florida remained free, but slaves could no longer earn their freedom simply by converting to Catholicism. They could still buy their freedom in other ways, however, such as by doing military service.

The growing number of blacks in Florida's military forces also worried the US government and white plantation owners. Slave uprisings were common in the Caribbean Islands. It seemed to the Americans that if revolts spread to Florida, the black militia would not be able to put them down.

Over the next 30 years, the US government put pressure on Spain to give up Florida. In the War of 1812, the United States finally ended British attempts to gain influence over North America. After the war, US troops began to make advances into Florida. They hoped to drive out the Spanish.

Spain could not afford to defend Florida. Within a few years, the Spaniards were ready to leave. They insisted that Florida's free black citizens must remain free under US control. The US government and many white Americans did not agree. They feared an **alliance** between Florida's Africans and Native Americans. The stage was set for war.

This drawing shows a Seminole village in Florida in the 1830s.

WHO WERE THE REBELS?

The rebels were made up of Native Americans called the Seminole and a group of freed and runaway slaves known as the Black Seminole.

The Seminole belonged to a branch of the Creek nation of Georgia and Alabama. The Creek first met Europeans when Hernando de Soto invaded their territory in 1538. As more European settlers arrived in North America, the native

Benjamin Hawkins (black coat) was the US government agent among the Creek.

This group of Seminole was photographed in the 1930s.

peoples who lived closest to the coast suffered the worst through warfare and disease. The Creek lived far enough inland to avoid the initial wave of European settlement. They supported English colonists in a struggle for control against the Spanish. However, like other native peoples, the Creek population was eventually greatly reduced by contact with European diseases against which the Creek had no natural resistance.

The Creek Move South

During the Revolutionary War, many Creek moved from southern Georgia to northern Florida to escape the fighting. From 1775, these Creek and the other peoples with whom they mixed in Florida started to be known as the Seminole.

A Huge Swamp

THE EVERGLADES OF SOUTHERN FLORIDA COVER MORE THAN 4,300 SQUARE MILES (11,100 SQ KM). IN THE MID-1800S, THE AREA WAS EVEN BIGGER. THE SHALLOW SUBTROPICAL SWAMP IS FULL OF MANGROVE TREES AND SAW GRASS. WHILE IT IS MORE THAN 50 MILES (80 KM) WIDE, THE SWAMP IS RARELY MORE THAN 1 FOOT (0.3 M) DEEP.

The Everglades has both open expanses of swampland and patches of thick forest.

The name of this new branch of the Creek probably came from the Creek word *simanó-li*, which means "runaway" or "**separatist**." Some experts think the word may instead have come from the Spanish word *cimarrón*, which means "wild."

Life in the Everglades

From northern Florida, some Seminole moved farther south to the Everglades. This was a huge, shallow swamp in the middle of southern Florida. The Seminole learned how to adapt to the swampy conditions. They lived in a special kind of house called a "chickee." Built from logs, the chickee had a living platform

that was raised above the damp ground. It had no walls, which allowed cooling breezes to lessen the intense heat. The Seminole grew corn, beans, melons, and squash. They also hunted and fished for food, and gathered nuts, berries, and roots.

The remote Everglades protected the Seminole from the outside world. Once the Seminole were settled there, they were almost immediately joined by escaped slaves and freed African Americans. People from other Native American groups also soon joined them.

This modern illustration shows Seminole "chickees" in the Everglades. →

These refugees were all escaping wars between European settlers and groups of Native Americans farther to the north. The Seminole welcomed the newcomers. The new arrivals soon adopted the life of the Seminole. The African Americans became known as the Black Seminole, although the two groups remained different.

Living in Harmony

The Black Seminole lived in villages close to the Seminole. They paid the Seminole **tribute**, a tax in the form of crops and animals. In exchange, the Black Seminole were allowed to live and trade with the Seminole. The two groups also **intermarried**.

A Seminole hunter named Charley Cypress in the Everglades in the 1930s.

Black Seminole culture was different from that of the Seminole. Many Black Seminole followed their own African version of Christianity, for example. They also spoke their own language, which modern experts call Afro-Seminole Creole. This was a mixture of Seminole and African languages, so the two groups could communicate easily. The Seminole spoke a language related to languages spoken by many native peoples in the Southeastern states.

A Threat?

By the 1820s, historians believe there were around 800 Black Seminole living with the Seminole. Both groups were highly **militaristic**. They had firearms, and they were ready to fight to defend themselves from attack. All the Seminole wanted to live independently. However, white expansion into Florida soon made that difficult. Whites began to **encroach** on Seminole land.

Seminole leaders discuss white encroachment with US general Andrew Jackson.

Andrew Jackson

Trained as a lawyer, Andrew Jackson (1767–1845) went on to have a successful military career. Jackson was later elected the seventh president of the United States. He served from 1829 to 1837. Jackson was the first president to come from west of the Appalachians, and much of his support came from the growing number of settlers in the West. In office, Jackson made changes that increased the number of male citizens who could take part in American politics by voting.

As president, Andrew Jackson dramatically increased the number of American men who could vote in elections.

One War Ends

In 1812, the United States went to war against Britain. The countries were fighting over international trade. An officer in the Tennessee militia, Major General Andrew Jackson, offered his services to the US government. The authorities sent him to fight the Creek. The Creek were allies of the British and were attacking white US settlements. Jackson defeated them so badly at the Battle of Tohopeka (Horseshoe Bend) in Alabama in 1814 that the Creek never again fought the whites. Next, Jackson headed to Louisiana, where British forces were threatening to capture New Orleans.

Jackson took charge of defense. The British surrendered at the Battle of New Orleans on January 8, 1815. Britain and the United States agreed to end the war. Neither side had been able to win a decisive victory over the other. Jackson headed back to Tennessee as a great US hero.

Another War Begins

In December 1817, the US government recalled Jackson to duty. Unrest on the frontier with Florida had grown worse. The government again sent Jackson to fight the Creek and the Seminole and to prevent Florida from offering a refuge for runaway slaves from the United States. Jackson decided to invade Spanish Florida.

Andrew Jackson (on horse) leads US forces at the Battle of New Orleans in 1815.

REBELLION!

The war between the United States and the Seminole that began in 1817 would be the first of three. Seminole resistance to white settlement would last over 40 years and cost the US government heavily.

General Andrew Jackson marched his men into Spanish Florida in March 1817. The campaign is known as the First Seminole War (1817–1818), although some historians date the start of the war from Jackson's fights with the Seminole's Creek allies in March 1814.

As Jackson's men advanced, the Seminole left their villages to try to stop them. Jackson's men found the Seminole villages left undefended and burned them down.

The Seminole took shelter in the swamps of the Everglades.

Jackson's advancing forces captured the city of Pensacola. The Spanish **garrison** there surrendered on May 28, 1817. Both the Spanish and the British governments expressed outrage at the US invasion of Florida.

The United States now controlled East Florida. The Spanish did not have the men or **resources** to push the US forces out. Neither could they stop runaway slaves crossing the border as Jackson demanded. In February 1819, Spain and the United States signed the Adams–Onís Treaty. Spain agreed to hand Florida to the United States. The treaty established the border between the United States and New Spain in the West.

Control of Florida passed to the United States in 1821. Early the next year, US officials estimated that there were about 22,000 Seminole in Florida. They were eager to move the Seminole to a **reservation**. The US government wanted the Seminole's rich farmland for white settlers.

The US government wanted to move the Seminole to Creek land in Arkansas.

In September 1823, US officials and the Seminole met at Moultrie Creek to sign a **treaty**. Under the terms of the treaty, the Seminole agreed to give up their land in northern Florida and move to a large reservation in central Florida. In return, the US government agreed to protect the Seminole from white settlers and to provide them with crops, farm animals, an interpreter, and a school for at least 20 years.

In 1828, Andrew Jackson was elected president of the United States. He had campaigned on a promise to remove all Native Americans from east of the Mississippi River. Jackson planned to force them to move to the West.

US soldiers camp outside a walled settlement in Picolata in northern Florida. ↓

→
Chief Coeehajo helped lead native warriors in the Second Seminole War.

In 1830, the US Congress passed the Indian Removal Act. Like other Native peoples in the east, the remaining Seminole were required to leave Florida for a newly created Indian territory in what is now Oklahoma.

A New Treaty

On May 9, 1832, Seminole chiefs and representatives of the US government met at Payne's Landing in Florida. They **negotiated** a treaty in great secrecy. The Seminole agreed to move if suitable land was found for them in the West. Later, the two sides would disagree about some of the terms that were agreed.

The US government wanted the Seminole to move to Creek land in what is now Arkansas and to return runaway slaves to their owners. The Seminole refused. Arkansas had a harsher climate than Florida. Also, although some Florida Seminole had originally come from the Creek, many came from different tribes with no connections to the Creek.

Seven Seminole chiefs traveled to inspect the new territory in Arkansas. They signed the Treaty of Payne's Landing there on March 28, 1833. When they got back to Florida, however, they claimed they had been forced to sign against their will. Now they refused to move. Some US Army officers at the signing agreed that the Seminole chiefs had been forced to sign. For its part, the US government insisted that the Seminole had 3 years to move from the time the treaty was originally discussed in May 1832. That meant the Seminole had to leave Florida in 1835.

This print shows a fort built by US soldiers on the St. John River in Florida in 1835.

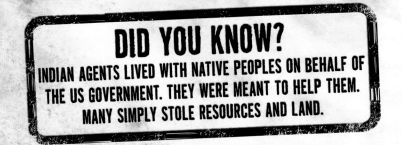

OSCEOLA

BORN BILLY POWELL, OSCEOLA (1804–1838) HAD A BRITISH FATHER AND A CREEK MOTHER. HE WAS RAISED BY HIS MOTHER. AFTER ANDREW JACKSON DEFEATED THE CREEK IN 1814, OSCEOLA MOVED TO FLORIDA. IN 1836, THE YOUNG MAN BECAME ADVISOR TO MICANOPY, THE CHIEF OF THE SEMINOLE. OSCEOLA LED RESISTANCE TO US FORCES. IN SEPTEMBER 1837, OSCEOLA WAS CAPTURED WHEN HE WAS TRICKED INTO ATTENDING PEACE TALKS. HE DIED IN FORT MOULTRIE, CHARLESTON, MOST LIKELY FROM AN INFECTION.

Osceola was the main leader of Seminole resistance to US forces in the 1830s.

The Second Seminole War

The deadline for the Seminole to move came and went. They stayed where they were. Wiley Thompson, the government agent responsible for making the Seminole move, immediately banned them from buying guns and ammunition. Meanwhile, volunteers from among the white American settlers in Florida formed militia groups. They were ready to fight the Seminole and force them to leave.

DECEPTION

THE CAPTURE OF OSCEOLA IN SEPTEMBER 1837 WAS ONE OF THE MOST CONTROVERSIAL INCIDENTS OF THE SEMINOLE WARS. OSCEOLA WAS INVITED TO PEACE TALKS IN ST. AUGUSTINE, FLORIDA. WHILE HE WAS THERE, GENERAL THOMAS JESUP SEIZED HIM. JESUP'S BEHAVIOR OUTRAGED MANY AMERICANS, BECAUSE OSCEOLA HAD GONE TO THE TALKS UNDER A FLAG OF **TRUCE**. THIS WAS A TRADITIONAL GUARANTEE OF SOMEONE'S SAFETY.

The Seminole had a new leader, Osceola. He led raids on white farms and settlements. The Seminole also attacked a military supply train, killing eight guards. On December 28, 1835, US Major Francis Dade marched his men from Fort Brooke to Fort King in Florida. Some 180

Sensational reports of the attack on Dade and his men appeared in newspapers across the United States.

The Seminole launch a surprise attack on a US fortification.

Seminole warriors attacked, killing 100 soldiers. Only one man survived the attack. That same day, Osceola and his men killed the government agent, General Wiley Thompson. This started a new war that would last for 7 years as a series of US generals tried and failed to defeat the Seminole.

Guerrilla Tactics

Throughout the Second Seminole War, the Seminole numbered fewer than 3,000 men. At their height, US forces in Florida were more than 30,000 troops. The Seminole used **guerrilla tactics**. Rather than fight large-scale battles, they attacked plantations and forts, killing civilians as well as soldiers. They used their knowledge of the swamps and forests to escape before the US forces could arrive to attack them.

FIGHTING AUTHORITY

The US government underestimated the Seminole. It also underestimated public opinion. Many Americans supported the right of the Seminole to stay in Florida.

The Second Seminole War was the longest, bloodiest, and most expensive campaign the US government ever waged against Native American groups. It was also a very unpopular war. Many Americans believed that the government was using **immoral** tactics to drive the Seminole out of Florida.

US troops burn the Seminole village of Pilak-li-ka-ha during the war.

Summer in Florida

During the summer, Florida was a hostile environment for US soldiers. It was hot, with high humidity caused by daily heavy rains. The few roads became impassable. Disease became widespread, as mosquitoes spread malaria. Typhoid was also common. So many soldiers became sick that for most of the Seminole Wars the army stopped fighting during the summer months.

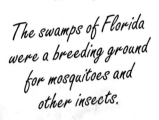

The swamps of Florida were a breeding ground for mosquitoes and other insects.

The Generals Fail

Andrew Jackson's rapid victory in the First Seminole War had misled US politicians and commanders. They expected little resistance from the Seminole. When the second war started in 1835, the US Army was very small. There were fewer than 7,500 men guarding 53 military posts spread across the vast territory of the expanding United States. If a need arose for more soldiers, the regular army was reinforced by militias and volunteer units organized by the states and territories.

↑ *Militia from South Carolina arrive at a ruined bridge on the Withlacoochee River.*

Successive Failures

A few days after the Dade **Massacre** and the death of Wiley Thompson, Seminole warriors stopped an attack by 75 soldiers led by General Duncan Clinch at Withlacoochee River. The Second Seminole War had begun. Its first months were marked by a string of US failures as the Army suffered defeat after defeat. In February 1836, General Gaines and 1,100 men were besieged at Camp Izard on the banks of the River Withlacoochee for more than a week before they retreated. The next month, General Winfield Scott arrived in Florida with 5,000 men. He spent a month looking unsuccessfully for the Seminole before giving up. The Seminole had hidden in the swamps. Next, Governor Richard K. Call led 1,000 men west of the Withlacoochee where he met strong resistance in the Battle of Wahoo Swamp on November 21, 1836.

General Thomas Jesup

The US attack improved in late 1836, when General Thomas Jesup assumed control. He organized a well-supplied campaign. Jesup built a series of forts and depots, including Fort Dade on the Withlacoochee River.

This US Army used trained bloodhounds to look for Seminole fighters in the swamps.

Jesup's efforts soon began to pay off. In March 1837, the Seminole's main chief, Micanopy, visited Fort Dade with other Seminole leaders to negotiate a surrender. The agreement collapsed in June, when slave catchers arrived to seize the Black Seminole. The Seminole left Fort Dade.

In September 1837, Jesup seized Osceola and other leaders who had attended more peace talks. The talks were carried out under a white flag of truce, which should have meant that neither side could act against the other. The deception turned public opinion against Jesup.

The Tide Turns

During the fall, Jesup brought in more than 9,000 troops to fight the Seminole. He also managed to persuade some of the Black Seminole to split from the Seminole by offering them freedom in the north. With so many troops, Jesup swept easily through Florida. On Christmas Day 1837, he fought the Seminole in the biggest clash of the war, the Battle of Okeechobee. The US Army suffered far more casualties than the Seminole, with 26 men killed and 112 wounded. Nevertheless, the US Army claimed victory.

←

A Seminole woman painted in 1834.

This modern illustration shows Seminole warriors attacking US militia.

Early in 1838, Jesup decided that it was pointless to chase the remaining Seminole into southern Florida. He advised Joel Poinsett, the Secretary of War, to stop the war, but Poinsett ignored his advice. Slaveholders in the South would not accept ending the war end until all the Seminole had been forced out of Florida. The fighting would continue for the next 4 years. Colonel Zachary Taylor had led US troops at Okeechobee. Now he replaced Jesup as commander. For the next 2 years, Taylor fought a defensive war with no real gains.

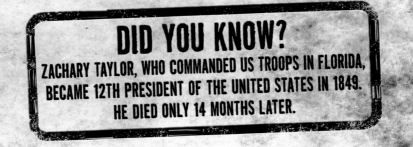

DID YOU KNOW?

ZACHARY TAYLOR, WHO COMMANDED US TROOPS IN FLORIDA, BECAME 12TH PRESIDENT OF THE UNITED STATES IN 1849. HE DIED ONLY 14 MONTHS LATER.

Thomas Jesup

General Thomas Jesup (1788–1860) commanded US troops in Florida during the Second Seminole War. His 52-year military career was one of the longest in US history. He was still in active service when he died at age 72. Jesup understood the importance of keeping troops supplied during a military campaign. He is sometimes known as the "Father of the Modern Quartermaster Corps," the army branch that organizes supplies.

By late 1838, opposition to the war had grown both in Congress and among the public. People admired the Seminole's defense of their land and they did not like the force and deception used by the US Army. Congress worried that the war was also becoming very expensive.

↓ US soldiers cross a lake during their search for the Seminole.

In spring 1839, the army sent its highest-ranking officer, Alexander Macomb, to negotiate a peace treaty with the Seminole. The discussions broke down in July. The Seminole no longer trusted the US government.

Stalemate Broken

The last two US commanders of the war took a new approach. Each summer, fighting halted in the Florida heat. The Seminole used this break to regroup and reorganize themselves, so US commanders decided to fight through the summer. Using canoes and small boats, the US army explored the Everglades where the Seminole were hiding. They forced captured Seminole to guide them. The Seminole were exhausted. They were running out of ammunition and food. Some were captured while others surrendered.

Alexander Macomb's talks with the Seminole failed to achieve a peace treaty.

In August 1842, the United States declared that the war was over. The army had lost around 1,500 men, most to disease. Some 30,000 volunteers had served in the campaign, and many had died. More than 4,000 Seminole were forcibly removed from Florida. The war had cost $30 million at a time when the whole federal budget for 1836 was just $25 million.

VICTORY AND LEGACY

When the Second Seminole War ended in 1842, there were only around 350 Seminole left in Florida. But they were determined to stay.

Despite 7 years of fighting, the Seminole remained undefeated. However, their numbers had been greatly reduced. Only a few hundred Seminole still lived in the Everglades. Meanwhile, more white pioneers moved farther south into Florida.

In 1842, the Armed Occupation Act granted any male **immigrant** who was prepared to serve in the

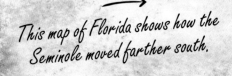

This map of Florida shows how the Seminole moved farther south.

In 1850, the US government passed a law to encourage settlers to turn swamp into farmland.

militia the right to claim 160 acres (65 ha) of land, provided he and his family lived on the land for at least 5 years. The population of Florida increased from 11,000 inhabitants in 1820 to 87,000 in 1850. Given the size of the state, however, these numbers alone did not threaten the existence of the surviving Seminole.

In September 1850, a new law changed everything. The US government passed the Swamp Land Act. The act returned all swamps and wetlands in federal ownership to states that agreed to drain them and turn them into agricultural land. The act was mainly intended to help develop the Everglades.

SWAMP LAND ACT OF 1850

ALTHOUGH THE MAIN TARGET OF THE SWAMP LAND ACT WAS THE FLORIDA EVERGLADES, IT ALSO AFFECTED WETLANDS OR SWAMPS IN ARKANSAS, ALABAMA, MISSISSIPPI, MISSOURI, AND 10 OTHER STATES. THE ACT ALLOWED INVESTORS TO DRAIN UNUSED AREAS TO TURN INTO FARMLAND. DRAINING THE WETLANDS DESTROYED THE NATURAL FLORA AND FAUNA.

THE ACT LED TO THE DESTRUCTION OF MUCH OF THE EVERGLADES, WHICH WAS REDUCED TO HALF ITS FORMER SIZE.

→

Less than half the Everglades survived the 1850 Swamp Land Act.

Florida now added land in the Everglades to the territory that could be claimed by white newcomers under the terms of the Armed Occupation Act.

The Third Seminole War (1855–1858)

The immediate result of the Swamp Land Act was the arrival of white settlers in the Everglades. Most had no expertise in managing or draining wetlands. The US government sent its own experts to figure out a plan. In December 1855, army engineers and **surveyors** arrived to study Big Cypress Swamp in the Everglades.

Big Cypress Swamp was home to the leader of the remaining Seminole, Chief Holata Micco. The Americans knew him as Chief Billy Bowlegs. Accounts vary as to what exactly happened. The army personnel had been ordered not to **provoke** the Seminole, but at some point the surveyors managed to destroy Chief Billy Bowleg's banana garden.

The chief was furious. When he confronted army commanders with what the surveyors had done, they did not apologize. Some historians now think that the vandalism was done deliberately to lure the Seminole into another war.

Conflict Begins

On the day after the chief's garden was destroyed, Seminole warriors attacked a US Army camp. They killed four soldiers and wounded four more. The US Army's response was to send 1,400 soldiers to fight the Seminole. Only about 100 Seminole warriors remained, so they were heavily outnumbered in the conflict.

→

Billy Bowlegs was angry when US soldiers destroyed his banana crop.

39

↑ *The destruction of Billy Bowlegs's banana crop caused the final Seminole war.*

Despite being outnumbered, the Seminole carried out a series of guerrilla attacks against US army bases. The US government responded by putting a **bounty** on the head of every Seminole. It offered bounty hunters $500 for every man, $250 for every woman, and $100 for every child. A Seminole who agreed to surrender could also claim the bounty.

Attempt at Peace

On August 21, 1856, the US government attempted to resolve the conflict by proposing a peace treaty with the Seminole and Creek tribes. It called for the Seminole to give up their land. The treaty wanted the Seminole to move to the West.

BILLY BOWLEGS

CHIEF HOLATA MICCO (C. 1810–1864) HAD MANY NAMES, INCLUDING BILLY BOWLEGS. THE NAME "BOWLEGS" DID NOT COME FROM RIDING A HORSE, BUT MAY HAVE BEEN AN ENGLISH VERSION OF THE NAME OF AN EARLIER SEMINOLE CHIEF, BOLEK. BILLY BOWLEGS LED THE SEMINOLE DURING THE SECOND SEMINOLE WAR, AFTER THE DEATHS OF OSCEOLA AND MICANOPY. HE SIGNED THE TREATY OF PAYNE'S LANDING IN 1832 BUT REFUSED TO LEAVE FLORIDA. THE CHIEF LIVED PEACEFULLY BETWEEN 1842 AND 1855, UNTIL THE THIRD WAR BROKE OUT AND HE AGAIN LED HIS WARRIORS.

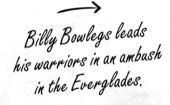

Billy Bowlegs leads his warriors in an ambush in the Everglades.

The Seminole rejected the terms of the treaty, and the war continued as a series of **skirmishes**. The last battle occurred in 1857, when the army burned Billy Bowlegs' camp and stole the Seminole's cattle, corn, and rice.

In 1858, the US government met with Billy Bowlegs. The circumstances of the meeting are not known, and accounts vary as to what happened. The result was that the Seminole chief finally agreed to leave Florida.

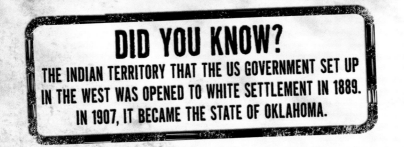
Some reports say that Billy Bowlegs only agreed to surrender after bounty hunters snatched his granddaughter. Other reports say that the chief agreed to move to Indian Territory (modern-day Oklahoma) in return for a payment of $8,000. Whichever story is true, on May 4, 1858, the chief left Florida. Along with 165 Seminole, he headed for a new life in the West, where he died a few years later. The Seminole Wars were at an end.

In the 1900s, Seminole still used traditional canoes to move around the lakes of the Everglades.

GROUP OF SEMINOLE BRAVES.

The Seminole never left Florida completely. They are proud of their long history of resistance.

The Seminole are proud that they were never defeated. The US government accepted in 1858 that it would never force all the Seminole to leave Florida. In the end, it simply left them alone. A small group of Seminole continued to live quietly in Big Cypress Swamp. Today approximately 3,500 Seminole live in Florida. They are the descendants of those few last Seminole and of Seminole who returned from the West. Florida had become a state in 1845. Some historians estimate that the Seminole Wars delayed statehood by around 30 years.

TIMELINE

1775 During the Revolutionary War, members of the Creek tribe move south into British Florida, where they become known as the Seminole.

1784 The Spanish recapture Florida from the British.

1790 Spain ends its Sanctuary Policy in Florida.

1812 **June 18:** The United States and Britain go to war in the War of 1812.

1814 **March 26:** US soldiers led by Andrew Jackson defeat the Seminole's Creek allies in the Battle of Tohopeka.

1815 **January 8:** Jackson becomes an American hero after defeating the British at New Orleans.

1817 **March:** Andrew Jackson marches into Florida, beginning the First Seminole War.

       May 8: Jackson captures Pensacola, bringing the Spanish territory of East Florida under US control.

1819 **February 22:** Spain and the United States sign the Adams–Onís Treaty, under which Spain agrees to leave Florida in 1821.

1823 **September:** The Seminole sign the Treaty of Moultrie Creek, agreeing to move to a reservation in central Florida.

1830 **May 28:** The Indian Removal Act authorizes the forced migration of native peoples west.

1832 **May 9:** Seminole leaders meet US government representatives at Payne's Landing to discuss a new treaty.

1833 **March 28:** Seminole leaders sign the treaty after visiting their proposed new lands. They later withdraw their agreement.

1835 **December 28:** The Second Seminole War begins when Seminole warriors kill 100 US soldiers and the US government agent Wiley Thompson.

1836 **November 1:** US and Seminole forces clash in the Battle of Wahoo Swamp.

1837 **September:** Osceola is captured during peace talks. He dies on January 20, 1838.

December 25: The biggest battle of the war is fought at Okeechobee.

1839 **Spring:** General Alexander Macomb tries but fails to negotiate a peace deal.

1842 **August 4:** The Armed Occupation Act grants land in Florida to settlers in return for service in the militia.

August 14: The US Army declares the Second Seminole War over.

1845 **March 3:** Florida achieves statehood.

1850 **September:** The Swamp Land Act is passed, encouraging the draining of the Florida Everglades.

1855 **December:** US Army surveyors in Big Cypress Swamp provoke the Seminole into a third war.

1858 **May 4:** Chief Billy Bowlegs and 165 Seminole head west from Florida, ending the Seminole Wars.

GLOSSARY

alliance: An agreement to work together for similar aims.

bounty: A sum paid for capturing or killing a person.

colonies: Regions that are governed by another country.

conquistadors: Spanish explorers in the Americas, who were usually seeking gold and other riches.

encroach: To intrude on someone else's property.

garrison: A group of soldiers stationed in a location in order to protect it.

guerrilla tactics: Describes methods used by small military forces, such as ambush or terrorism.

immigrant: Someone who has moved to live in a new area.

immoral: Not according to accepted ideas of good behavior.

intermarried: Married someone from another race or group.

massacre: The murder of many people in an attack.

militaristic: Being aggressive and ready to fight.

militias: Military forces raised from the civilian population.

negotiate: To agree to an arrangement through discussion.

plantations: Large farms on which crops are grown.

provoke: To push someone so that they react negatively.

refugees: People who are fleeing from danger or disaster.

reservation: A piece of land set aside for Native Americans.

resources: Materials that are useful for a purpose.

sanctuary: Safety from pursuit or danger.

separatist: Someone who wants to live apart from others.

skirmishes: Small-scale fighting.

surveyors: People who carefully measure a particular area of land.

treaty: A formal agreement between two states.

tribute: Payment made to a ruler as a sign of respect.

truce: A temporary halt in fighting.

FURTHER INFORMATION

Books

Frank, Andrew K.
The Seminole. History and Culture of Native Americans.
New York: Chelsea House Publications, 2010.

George, Gale.
Seminole. Spotlight on Native Americans. New York: PowerKids Press, 2016.

Gunderson, Megan M.
Andrew Jackson, 7th President of the United States. US Presidents.
Edina, MN: ABDO, 2011.

Sanford, William R.
Seminole Chief Osceola. Native American Chiefs and Warriors. Berkeley Heights, NJ: Enslow Publishers, 2013.

Websites

www.ducksters.com/history/ native_americans/seminole_ tribe.php
An overview of the Seminole in history and their lives today.

dos.myflorida.com/florida- facts/florida-history/ seminole-history/the- seminole-wars/
A detailed account of the Seminole Wars from the Florida Department of State.

kids.britannica.com/ comptons/article-9599580/ Seminole-Wars
A short summary of the Seminole Wars and their effects.

dos.myflorida.com/florida- facts/florida-history/ seminole-history/seminole- leaders/
Biographies of important Seminole leaders, including Osceola and Billy Bowlegs.

INDEX